ASIAN PEOPLE
Who Changed History

Adam Sutherland

WAYLAND

First published in 2013 by Wayland
Copyright © Wayland 2013

Wayland
338 Euston Road
London NW1 3BH

Wayland Australia
Hachette Children's Books
Level 17/207
Kent Street
Sydney, NSW 2000

Editor: Nicola Edwards
Designer: Tim Mayer, MayerMedia

A CIP catalogue record for this book is available from the
British Library.
ISBN 978 0 7502 7967 3

Wayland is a division of Hachette Children's Books, as
Hachette UK company

www.hachette.co.uk

Picture acknowledgements
The author and publisher would like to thank the
following for allowing their pictures to be reproduced
in this publication: Cover: Getty Images/David Hill;
title page: vipflash/Shutterstock.com; p4(t) Asianet-
Pakistan/ Shutterstock.com, (b) Audrey Burmakin/
Shutterstock.com; p5 Getty Images; p7 Shutterstock.
com; p8 Audrey Burmakin/Shutterstock.com p9
Getty Images; p10 SNEHIT/Shutterstock.com; p11
Getty Images; p12 U.S. National Archives and Records
Administration; p13 Hung Chung Chih/Shutterstock.
com; p14 Time & Life Pictures/Getty Images; p15
Sergey Goryachev/Shutterstock.com p16 Hung Chung
Chih/ Shutterstock.com; p17 National Geographic/
Getty Images; p18 vipflash/Shutterstock.com; p19
Paris Match via Getty Images; p20 Devin Patel/
Shutterstock.com; p21 Manoj Deka/Demotix/Demotix/
Press Association Images; p22 (mb) Olga Popova /
Shutterstock.com;

Words in **bold** can be found in the glossary on page 24.

Making History

Sarojini Naidu, India's first woman governor, campaigned for her country's independence through non-violent protest.

Asia is home to some of the world's earliest **civilizations**. From India to China and across the Himalayas, the continent has been home to turbulent tribes, bloody **conquerors**, freedom fighters and wise, **enlightened** holy men.

History making can be about forming countries out of **chaos**, creating new belief systems that **endure** for thousands of years, overcoming outstanding physical challenges, or putting personal life and **liberty** on the line to achieve something memorable and long-lasting.

This statue of Genghis Khan, commemorates the life of the warrior leader who conquered warring tribes and united Mongolia.

Making a difference

The history makers included in this book couldn't be more different – from the extreme bloodshed of Genghis Khan (page 8) and Mao Tse-Tung (page 12), to the non-violent resistance of Gandhi (page 10), Sarojini Naidu (page 14) and the Dalai Lama (page 18), and the **contemplation** and learning of Confucius (page 7) and Buddha (page 6). But all have made their mark on Asian history – whether it was by building an empire, uniting its people, speaking out against injustice, or establishing new belief systems.

A place in history

Some people make history through their **phenomenal** achievements – like mountaineer Tenzing Norgay (page 16), who was the first man to conquer Mount Everest. Or architect IM Pei (page 17), whose designs – including the Louvre's thought-provoking glass and steel pyramid – have earned his place in the history books.

The magic ingredients

What does it take to become a history maker? Undoubtedly a strong will, unshakeable self-belief, and a refusal to give up until the job is done – from the building of an empire, the foundation of a new religion, a climb to the top of the world, or independence for one's countrymen.

The history of Asia is as fascinating as it is confusing, as enlightened as it is brutal. And all our entries here have played their part in making it unique.

Tenzing Norgay on the summit of Everest. No pictures exist of fellow climber Sir Edmund Hillary on the top of the mountain as Norgay didn't know how to work the camera!

Gautama Buddha
The Enlightened One

Gautama grew up in a palace in Nepal, sheltered from the outside world. However, so the story goes, he went out riding one day, and saw an old man, then a sick man, then a corpse. The realities of old age, disease and death made the young prince begin his search for enlightenment.

On a quest

Gautama and five companions visited many well-known teachers, **fasting**, learning to **meditate**, and discovering many different religious beliefs. Through meditation, he decided that a 'Middle Way', between pleasure and pain, was the true path to enlightenment.

Discovering Buddhism

Gautama told disciples he had discovered the cause of human suffering, and the steps needed to eliminate it – the 'Four Noble Truths' at the heart of Buddhist teaching. Master these truths, he explained, and a state of pure happiness and fulfilment, or Nirvana, would be achieved. Gautama spent the remaining 45 years of his life travelling, and spreading the word of enlightenment.

Full name: Siddhartha Gautama

Born: 583 BCE in Kapilavastu, Nepal

Died: 483 BCE in Theravada, India

Honours and achievements: Gautama's teachings are followed today by around 350 million people. That's about 6 per cent of the world's population.

Interesting fact: Buddha means 'enlightened one' or 'awakened one'.

MAKING HISTORY

Gautama's quest created a belief system and a way of life for many people that still exists today.

Buddha sits among his disciples. The earliest Buddhist art dates back to the first century BCE.

Confucius
Respected thinker

Confucius was a Chinese teacher, politician and philosopher who lived during the Spring and Autumn Period (77-481 BCE) of Chinese history. His **philosophy** was based on traditional Chinese beliefs, emphasising the importance of family, mutual respect, justice and sincerity. His best-known concept is: 'Do not do to others what you do not want done to yourself'.

Youthful teachings

Education was very important to the young Confucius. It's believed he studied under Daoist Master Lao Dan, and then built his own group of followers. Confucius taught the Six Arts: archery, **calligraphy**, chariot racing, computation (maths), music and ritual.

Creating history

Confucius believed he was a 'transmitter' of learning — merely passing on thoughts to his students. However, his **groundbreaking**, original beliefs and teachings — which became Confucianism — still exist and thrive today all over the world.

Full name: Kong Qiu

Born: 551 BCE

Died: 479 BCE

Honours and achievements: A collection of Confucius' sayings and ideas were collected in an ancient Chinese text called the Analects.

Interesting fact: Asteroid 7853 was named 'Confucius' in his honour.

Confucius is said to have been born into the 'Shi' class, between the aristocracy and the common people.

> " He who learns but does not think is lost. He who thinks but does not learn is in great danger. "
>
> *Confucius*

Genghis Khan
Empire Builder

Full name: Temujin

Born: around 1155 in Delüün Boldog, northern Mongolia

Died: around 1227 in Khentii Aimag, northern Mongolia

Honours and achievements: Regarded as the founding father of Mongolia. Created a unified empire, promoted religious tolerance, introduced the country's first legal system.

Interesting fact: A river was diverted over his grave to make the site impossible to find.

Building an army

By the age of 20, Temujin had built an army of 20,000 men. His plan was to conquer all the warring tribes and unite Mongolia under his rule. His military tactics were ahead of their time – he employed spies to gain intelligence on his enemies, used a system of smoke signals to plot his army's advance, and ensured his soldiers were well equipped (with bow, arrows, shield and dagger), well fed, and had access to the best medical supplies.

Genghis Khan passed laws protecting the environment and provided advancement based on ability, not birthright.

Temujin was born in a land of feuding tribes, who often fought to the death for power and territory in the mountains of northern Mongolia. Relations with neighbouring tribes were often bad. Temujin's wife, Borte, was kidnapped by the Merkit tribe shortly after their marriage, his father was murdered by the Tatar tribe, and Temujin himself was captured in a raid and was only freed by a family friend who lived in the enemy camp.

A time for peace

A disagreement with Shah Muhammad, the leader of the Khwarizm Dynasty that included Iraq and Afghanistan, led to a bloody two-year advance through the Shah's cities that ended his rule by 1221. At this time, the war-like Khan turned his attention to creating a peaceful, fair and law-abiding empire — with a new system of laws, protection of the environment and the freedom to worship without fear of **persecution**. After his death in 1227, Khan's four sons ruled his empire for many years.

Genghis Khan orders a prisoner to be flogged. Khan once told an enemy: "If you had not committed great sins, God would not have sent a punishment like me upon you."

Conquering Mongolia

By 1206 Temujin had defeated the powerful Naiman tribe, and taken control of central and eastern Mongolia. Rival tribal leaders gave him the title Genghis Khan, meaning 'universal ruler'. As food and resources grew short in Khan's empire, he led his army towards the kingdom of Xi Xia and the plentiful rice fields of the Jin Dynasty in China.

MAKING HISTORY

Genghis Khan built the largest empire in the world, conquering and uniting tribes in Asia from China to Turkey, thanks to his brilliant and often groundbreaking military tactics.

Mohandas Gandhi
Pioneer of non-violence

Gandhi lived simply and dressed in clothes that he made himself, using a spinning wheel.

> " You must be the change you want to see in the world. "
>
> *Mohandas Gandhi*

Full name: Mohandas Karamchand Gandhi

Born: 2 October 1869 in Porbandar, Gujarat, India

Died: 30 January 1948 in New Delhi, India

Honours and awards: TIME magazine's Man of the Year (1930), TIME magazine '25 Top Political Icons of All Time' (2011), his birthday was declared an 'International Day of Non-Violence' by the United Nations (2007).

Interesting fact: Nominated five times for the Nobel Peace Prize between 1937-1948 but never won.

Gandhi was born in the west of India, in a small state ruled by a prince. His father, Karamchand, was the prince's chief advisor. After he left school, Gandhi persuaded his family to let him go to London to study law. He passed his exams and found work in South Africa. At the time, both India and South Africa were part of the British Empire, and ruled by Great Britain.

Campaigning in South Africa

While in South Africa, Gandhi witnessed racial prejudice for the first time. He was determined to speak up for people with no economic or political power. He campaigned for voting rights for the Indian workers living there, organised petitions to raise support, and even started a political party. Gandhi was put in jail for his actions, but eventually he succeeded in many of his aims.

Back to India

In 1915 Gandhi returned to India. He witnessed great poverty, but was impressed by the lives of villagers in the countryside and decided to live a simpler life himself. He campaigned for poor workers and farmers, and for people from the lowest 'caste', or class, in India society. He also called for peace between Hindus and Muslims.

Non-violent protest

From 1921, Gandhi led the Indian National Congress, campaigning against British rule. He used a new method of action called 'strength in truth' and called for people to refuse to obey the law. This is known as civil disobedience. Although he insisted that protest should never be violent, he was often jailed for his actions. After the Second World War, the British government at last agreed to Indian independence. Unfortunately, there were violent disagreements between Hindus and Muslims, and eventually two separate states were created – India and Pakistan. In 1948, Gandhi was shot and killed by a Hindu **extremist**, but his ideas and actions live on.

Gandhi walks among commuters in a London street while on a visit as leader of the Indian Independence Movement to a conference in 1931.

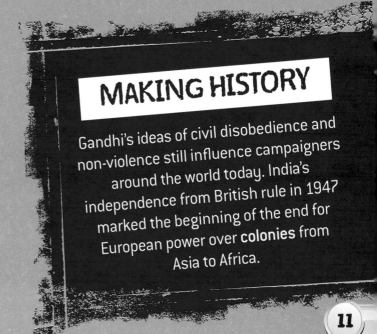

MAKING HISTORY

Gandhi's ideas of civil disobedience and non-violence still influence campaigners around the world today. India's independence from British rule in 1947 marked the beginning of the end for European power over **colonies** from Asia to Africa.

Mao Tse-tung
Communist revolutionary

Mao Tse-tung grew up on a small three-acre farm that had been in his family for generations. His father was a wealthy grain dealer, and by 13 Mao was working alongside him in the fields. But a life on the farm was not Mao's destiny – at 17 he left home to go to school in Changsha, the state capital. By 1911, the Xinhua Revolution began against the Chinese monarchy, and Mao joined the Revolutionary Army.

Full name: Mao Tse-tung

Born: 26 December 1893 in Shaoshan, Hunan Province, China

Died: 9 September 1976 in Beijing, China

Honours and achievements: Unified China, improved women's rights, funded important infrastructure projects, reformed land ownership giving power to individual famers.

Interesting fact: More than 6 billion copies of the book 'Quotations of Chairman Mao' were published.

A young Mao Tse-tung addresses his communist followers.

Surviving oppression

Mao learned about the Russian Revolution, and the formation of the **communist** Soviet Union, and by 1921 he became one of the first members of the Chinese Communist Party. By 1934, the communists controlled several regions of Jiangxi Province. The Chinese president Chiang Kaishek was afraid of their growing popularity and sent troops to arrest them. Mao led his supporters on the 'Long March' across the mountains to escape – more than 70,000 of the original 100,000 members died on the journey.

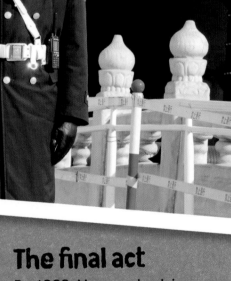

A guard stands in Beijing's Tiananmen Square, overlooked by a giant portrait of Mao.

The rise to power

When Japan invaded China in 1937, Chiang Kaishek was forced to seek help from Mao, who proved himself a gifted military leader. Their truce was shortlived, and by 1949, Mao announced the formation of the People's Republic of China, forcing Chiang into exile. Mao introduced many positive changes, including improved health care, better access to education, and fairer distribution of land.

The dark side

Not all Mao's policies were a success, however. His plans to improve agricultural and industrial production went disastrously wrong, and millions died of hunger from 1959-1961. Critics were imprisoned or killed, and Mao himself was edged out of power by his rivals.

The final act

By 1966, Mao was back in power and launched the Cultural Revolution to enforce communism throughout China, leading his country through fear, **intimidation** and murder. Schools were closed, intellectuals were sent to work on labour camps, and much of China's cultural heritage was destroyed. The man who laid the foundations for China's late 20th century development was as much a monster as he was a genius.

Sarojini Naidu
Independence activist

Sarojini Naidu was a **child prodigy** who came first in an entrance exam for Madras University at just 12 years old. Her father wanted Naidu to follow him into mathematics, but the youngster preferred poetry, and starting scribbling verses in her exercise books when she was stuck on complex algebra problems. At 13, Naidu wrote a poem called 'The Lady of the Lake' that was 1,300-lines long.

Indian pride

After spending time at university in England, Naidu returned to India and became involved in her country's struggle for independence. She also campaigned for women's rights, travelling from village to village, giving talks on **nationalism** and the rights of women. After meeting Gandhi in 1916, she put all her energies into securing India's freedom.

In prison

In 1917 Naidu helped to establish the Women's Indian Association. She travelled to the United States in 1925 to spread Gandhi's beliefs about non-violent protest, and when he was arrested, Naidu led the movement until his release. She even spent time behind bars herself for protesting against British rule. After India gained independence, she became the country's first woman governor.

Full name: Sarojini Naidu

Born: 13 February 1879 in Hyderabad, India

Died: 2 March 1949 in Lucknow, Utter Pradesh, India

Honours and achievements: President of the Indian National Congress. First woman to become governor of Uttar Pradesh state.

Interesting fact: Naidu's birthday is celebrated as Women's Day across India.

Naidu's support of Gandhi led her to devote her life to the cause of Indian independence.

Emperor Hirohito
Transformative leader

Hirohito led Japan from 1926 until his death in 1989, reigning over attempted military coups, foreign invasions, world war and eventually peaceful rebuilding and economic strength.

Military power

When Hirohito came to power after the death of his father, Japan was a powerful world economy. Leaders of the Japanese Army and Navy wanted to lead the country, protecting Japan from attack and expanding its borders. Hirohito approved invasions to Manchuria in 1931 and parts of China in 1937, and formed the Axis Powers with Germany and Italy in 1940.

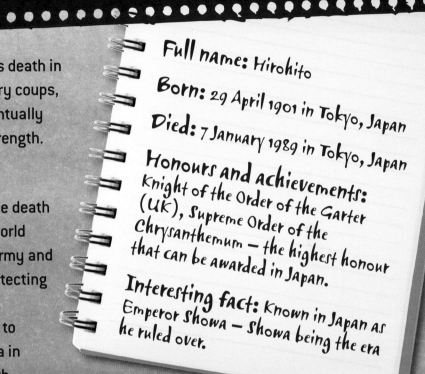

Full name: Hirohito

Born: 29 April 1901 in Tokyo, Japan

Died: 7 January 1989 in Tokyo, Japan

Honours and achievements: Knight of the Order of the Garter (UK), Supreme Order of the Chrysanthemum — the highest honour that can be awarded in Japan.

Interesting fact: Known in Japan as Emperor Showa — Showa being the era he ruled over.

Going to war

In December 1941 Japan attacked the US fleet in Pearl Harbor, forcing America to enter World War II. By 1944, Hirohito realised Japan was losing the War and, during the Battle of Saipan, encouraged Japanese civilians to commit suicide rather than be taken prisoner. Over 10,000 Japanese people took their own lives.

Rebuilding the country

Following the Japanese surrender, Hirohito continued as Emperor, helping to rebuild his country's devastated economy, and meeting world leaders to resurrect Japan's image overseas. By his death, Japan had the world's second-largest economy.

Emperor Hirohito led his country into a disastrous war, then to a prosperous peace.

Tenzing Norgay
Conqueror of Everest

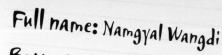

Full name: Namgyal Wangdi

Born: May 1914 in Tengboche, Khumbu, Nepal (exact date of birth unknown)

Died: 9 May 1986 in Darjeeling, West Bengal, India

Honours and achievements: George Medal (UK), and the Order of the Star of Nepal, 1st Class. Named by TIME magazine as one of the 100 Most Influential People of the 20th Century.

Interesting fact: As a child his name was changed to Ngawang Tenzin Norbu on the advice of a local Buddhist monk.

Reaching the summit

During the 1930s, Norgay carried supplies for three failed attempts on Everest. In 1947 and 1952 he tried and failed again, but reached a then-record height of 8,600m. In 1953 he was part of John Hunt's expedition of over 400 people. Along with Edmund Hillary, whose life he had saved earlier in the expedition, Norgay braved ice walls and sheer rock faces to reach the summit and make history.

A statue of Norgay in Darjeeling, India, where he lived in a Sherpa community. He said of his life "It has been a long road...From a bearer of loads to a wearer of a coat with rows of medals."

Tenzing Norgay is famous for being one of the first men to stand on top of the world. He reached the summit of Mount Everest on 29 May 1953 with the New Zealand climber Edmund Hillary.

Early days

Norgay was a survivor. The 11th of 13 children (most died young), he twice ran away from home as a child, and even spent time living as a Buddhist monk, before finally settling in the Sherpa community of Darjeeling aged 19.

IM Pei
Visionary architect

IM Pei went to school in Shanghai and studied architecture at some of the United States' most prestigious universities. His modernist style, and his combination of traditional and progressive designs have earned him the title of one of the greats of modern architecture.

Independent thinker

The young Pei disagreed with his university's focus on Beaux-Arts architecture, so focused instead on the work of groundbreaking designers such as Le Corbusier. By 1955 he had set up his own company, IM Pei & Associates. After President Kennedy's assassination in 1963, Pei was selected as chief architect for the John F Kennedy Library in Massachusetts.

I M Pei at the Louvre, with the glass pyramid he designed above him.

Full name: Ieo Ming Pei

Born: 26 April 1917 in Canton (Guangzhou), China.

Honours and achievements: Pritzker Architecture Prize (1983), known as the Nobel Prize of architecture. Also the AIA Gold Medal (1979), and a Lifetime Achievement Award from the National Design Museum (2003).

Interesting fact: Pei was the first foreign architect to work on the Louvre.

Causing controversy

In 1981 Pei designed a glass and steel pyramid for the courtyard of the Louvre museum in Paris, with an inverted pyramid underground serving as the entrance hall. Pei estimated that 90 per cent of Parisians opposed his design, but with government support he completed the project and turned public opinion in his favour. The Louvre pyramid has become one of Pei's greatest achievements.

The 14th Dalai Lama
Campaigner for a free Tibet

The 14th Dalai Lama was chosen as head monk of Tibetan Buddhism at just two years old. According to tradition, Dalai Lamas are selected as reincarnations of their predecessor. Spiritual leaders followed signs to a humble farmhouse in rural Takster, and returned the child — one of seven brothers and sisters — to the holy palace where he was ordained as a monk.

Full name: Lhamo Thondup

Born: 6 July 1935 in Takster, Qinghai, Tibet

Honours and achievements: Nobel Peace Prize winner (1989), Congressional Gold Medal (2007) — the highest civilian award in the US.

Interesting fact: Dalai Lamas have been leading Tibetan Buddhists since 1391.

The 14th Dalai Lama speaks to supporters in Berlin in 2008.

Life in religion
The young boy was renamed Jetsun Jamphel Ngawang Lobsang Yeshe Tenzin Gyatso (meaning Holy Lord, Gentle Glory, Compassionate, Defender of the Faith, Ocean of Wisdom) and started his monastic education at just six years old. At the age of 15, on 17 November 1950, he was formally recognised as the 14th Dalai Lama.

Conflict with China
The Dalai Lama spent most of his first decade in charge trying to avoid a military takeover of Tibet by Chinese forces. Tibet lies between India and China, but has long fought wars of

independence with its larger neighbour. By 1959, the Dalai Lama had to flee to India when Chinese forces invaded his homeland. He has been based in India ever since.

Spreading the word

Through high-profile meetings with presidents, prime ministers and world religious leaders, the Dalai Lama has kept the plight of Tibet and displaced Tibetans on the world's agenda. He has also spoken in front of the United Nations General Assembly calling for the protection of the Tibetan people.

> " The path of non-violence is our irrevocable commitment... It is important that there be no departure at all from this path. "
>
> *14th Dalai Lama*

The Dalai Lama is welcomed to India in 1959 after being forced to flee Tibet.

Freedom for Tibet

Despite approaching the age of 80, the Dalai Lama continues to fight and campaign for a free Tibet. His five-point plan includes the creation of a 'zone of peace' to protect Tibet's culture and environment from aggressive development by the Chinese government. The Dalai Lama's voice continues to be heard.

MAKING HISTORY

The Dalai Lama's strength of personality and strict belief in non-violence has brought worldwide support for the plight of Tibet and the Tibetan people.

Indira Gandhi
Groundbreaking prime minister

Gandhi's rule led to significant increases in economic, political and military power in India, strengthening its profile both at home and abroad.

prime minister, as well as the only woman to have held the position. Gandhi concentrated on making her country's economy less dependent on foreign aid.

Economic improvements

One of Gandhi's great successes was the Green Revolution, an agricultural policy that gave a huge boost to some of India's poorest inhabitants. In 1984, after she had ordered the army to break up a Sikh siege at the Golden Temple in Amritsar, she was murdered by two of her Sikh bodyguards. Nearly 3,000 Sikhs died in rioting following news of her death.

As the only child of India's first independent prime minister, Jawaharlal Nehru, Gandhi was destined for power. However, she turned down the prime minister's job when her father died, only agreeing to take office when his successor also passed away.

Strong rule

Gandhi ruled from 1966-1977, and from 1980 to 1984, making her India's second longest-serving

Full name: Indira Priyadarshini Nehru

Born: 19 November 1917 in Allahabad, United Provinces, India

Died: 31 October 1984 in New Delhi

Honours and achievements: Voted India's greatest prime minister (2001) in a poll by India Today. Named 'Woman of the Millennium' in a BBC poll (1999).

Interesting fact: Studied history at Oxford University, but her degree was interrupted by World War II.

Arundhati Roy
Human rights campaigner

Arundhati Roy's Booker-Prize-winning **novel** The God of Small Things (1998) turned her into a global superstar. In the years following the book's publication she has dedicated herself to raising public awareness on a variety of humanitarian causes – from the threat of nuclear weapons to the destruction of areas of natural beauty.

Causing controversy

The writer has used her famous name to shine a light on causes that she feels strongly about. Roy is a spokesperson for the anti-globalization movement (opposing the rise of powerful global organisations who put profit before working standards and environmental protection). She has also criticised India's nuclear weapons programme.

Global reach

Roy has contributed royalties from her writing to literacy programmes in India's most deprived regions. She has also used her non-fiction writing to bring the world's attention to activities such as the controversial Narmada Dam Project in Gujarat, India, which displaced thousands of families living in the region. Roy continues to fight for people less fortunate than herself.

Arundhati Roy addresses a meeting in India. Her non-fiction work often supports environmental causes.

Full name: Arundhati Roy

Born: 24 November 1961 in Shillong, Meghalaya, India

Honours and achievements: Lannan Foundation's Cultural Freedom Award (2002), named 'Woman of Peace' at the Global Exchange Human Rights Awards (2003), Sydney Peace Prize (2004).

Interesting fact: Roy studied architecture at the University of Delhi.

Other Asian People who Changed History

Corazon Aquino (1933-2009)

First woman president of the Philippines, and first female president in Asia. Aquino's politician husband Benigno was a strong critic of the dictatorship of President Marcos. After Benigno's assassination in 1983, Aquino entered politics herself and became leader of the opposition. In 1986 she led the People Power Revolution that removed Marcos from power and brought democracy back to the Philippines.

Jalal-ud-Din Mohammed Akbar (1556-1605)

During Akbar's reign he laid the foundations for modern India, strengthening the country against foreign threats, introducing a new era of religious tolerance between Muslims and Hindus, and encouraging the growth of arts and culture.

Rabindranath Tagore (1861-1941)

A child prodigy who was writing poetry at 8, and published his first book of short stories at 16, Kolkata-born Tagore was the first non-European to win the Nobel Prize in Literature in 1913. He introduced Indian culture to the West and, thanks to his huge body of work, is regarded as the most important creative artist his country has ever produced.

Rani Lakshmibai (1835-1858)

Queen of Jhansi, Lakshmibai was a leading figure in the Indian Rebellion of 1857, and a symbol of resistance to the British East India Company's rule. When her son died, she adopted a child to be her heir. The British would not accept the new heir, sparking a short but fierce conflict between British and Indian forces. Lakshmibai bravely joined the fight, and was killed in battle.

Jawaharlal Nehru (1889-1964)

A follower of Gandhi, Nehru was the first Prime Minister of India and ruled the country from its independence in 1947 until his death. A lawyer and graduate of Cambridge University in England, Nehru is credited with establishing India as a modern, democratic nation, and was the author of the Indian Declaration of Independence (1929).

Benazir Bhutto (1953-2007)

A former prime minister of Pakistan who led her country between 1988-90 and 1993-96. The eldest daughter of former Pakistani prime minister, Zulfikar Ali Bhutto, she became the first Pakistani woman to lead a major political party when she became head of the centre-left PPP at just 29. Bhutto was assassinated in 2007 while she was campaigning for a third term in office.

Timeline

Legacy

c.534 BCE Buddha embarks on path to enlightenment

1206 Genghis Khan conquers central and east Asia

1913 Rabindranath Tagore wins the Nobel Prize in Literature

1947 Jawaharlal Nehru becomes India's first prime minister

1948 Mohandas Gandhi assassinated

1949 Mao Tse-tung forms the People's Republic of China

1950 Lhamo Thondup is officially recognised as the 14th Dalai Lama

1953 Tenzing Norgay reaches the summit of Mount Everest

1959 14th Dalai Lama flees Tibet after Chinese invasion

1966 Mao Tse-tung launches the Cultural Revolution; Indira Gandhi becomes prime minister of India

1981 IM Pei designs the Louvre's glass pyramid

1984 Indira Gandhi assassinated

1986 Corazon Aquino comes to power in the Philippines

1988 Benazir Bhutto become prime minister of Pakistan

1989 14th Dalai Lama is awarded the Nobel Peace Prize

2003 Arundhati Roy named 'Woman of Peace' at the Global Exchange Human Rights Awards

2007 Benazir Bhutto assassinated

The legacies of the history makers in this book live on, not only in their achievements but also through the work of their followers:

The Dalai Lama Trust
http://www.dalailamatrust. org
Founded in 2009 to support the activities of individuals or institutions working for the welfare of the Tibetan people, and the advancement of the culture and heritage of Tibet.

The Tzu Chi Foundation
http://www.tzuchi.org
Established in 1966 in Taiwan by Buddhist master Cheng Yen. The Foundation aims to provide medical care, education and humanitarian support around the world.

The Gandhi World Hunger Fund
http://www. gandhiworldhungerfund.org/
Founded in 2008 by Arun Gandhi, fifth generation grandson of Mohandas Gandhi. Its mission is to provide food, clothing, shelter and education to needy children and their families, in areas affected by civil wars and natural disasters.

Glossary

Index

Beaux-Arts architecture A style of architecture taught at the École des Beaux-Arts in Paris.

calligraphy The art of producing beautiful handwriting.

chaos A state of total confusion.

child prodigy A child whose abilities far exceed what would be usual for someone of their age.

civilization An organized and well developed human society.

colony A country controlled by another more powerful country, often far away.

communist Someone who believes in communism, a way of organising a country so that all the means of production, such as farms and factories, belong to everyone.

conqueror Someone who takes control of a country or its people.

contemplation Serious, quiet thought for a period of time.

displaced Forced out of one's original country or region.

endure To last, remain.

enlightened Understanding the truth about human existence.

extremist A person with extreme religious or political views, whose actions are generally seen as unreasonable and unacceptable.

fasting Going without food for a certain length of time, usually a few days.

groundbreaking Completely new or different from what has gone before.

infrastructure The systems and services of a country, such as transport and power supplies, that help it work effectively.

intimidation To frighten or threaten someone in order to make them do something against their will.

inverted Upside-down

liberty Freedom

meditate To think calm thoughts, usually as part of a religious activity.

military coup The sudden removal of a government by a country's military leaders.

nationalism A nation's wish or attempts to be politically independent.

persecution Unfair or cruel treatment over a period of time because of race, religion or political beliefs.

phenomenal Extremely successful or special

philosophy A way of understanding and studying the world.

progressive Developing or happening gradually

History Makers

Contents of all titles in the series: